MĀTṚCEṬA'S HYMN TO THE BUDDHA

An English Rendering of the Śatapañcāśatka

By Ven S Dhammika

BUDDHIST PUBLICATION SOCIETY

Kandy   1989   Sri Lanka

First published in 1989
Buddhist Publication Society
PO Box 61
54, Sangharaja Mawatha
Kandy, Sri Lanka
©1989 by Ven S Dhammika

I S B N 955-24-0050-3

Note on frontispiece:
Gandhara Buddha, 5th Century AD
in the Indian Museum, Calcutta

Printed by
OCEAN COLOUR PRINTING PTE LTD
SINGAPORE

THE WHEEL PUBLICATION No. 360/361.

INTRODUCTION

For centuries people have stood in awe of the Buddha and his attainments and have strived to express their feelings in stone and bronze and with brush and ink. Some have been moved by what the Buddha said, its logical consistency, its scope and its humanism. Others have been inspired by the personality of the Lord himself, his manner and conduct, and even his physical form. The joyful faith and appreciation that is evoked on recollecting the Buddha's personality and singing his praise gives such people the strength they need to walk the Path. For them the Dhamma comes alive through the life and example of the Buddha.

Such a person was the poet Mātṛceṭa. He was born in India in about the first century A.D., and was converted from Hinduism to Buddhism by the great philosopher Āryadeva. He wrote about a dozen works, some of such beauty that he came to be regarded as one of India's greatest poets.[1] I-tsing, the Chinese pilgrim who travelled through India in the seventh century A.D., says of Mātṛceṭa's poems:

> These charming compositions are equal in beauty to the heavenly flowers and the high principles which they contain rival in dignity the lofty peaks of a mountain. Consequently in India all who compose hymns imitate his style, considering him the father of literature. Even men like Bodhisattvas Asaṅga and Vasubandhu admire him greatly. Throughout India everyone who becomes a

monk is taught Mātṛceṭa's two hymns as soon as they can recite the five and ten precepts.

I-tsing also recounts a beautiful legend that was told about the poet indicating his wide popularity:

> While the Buddha was living, he was once, while instructing his followers, wandering in a wood among the people. A nightingale in the wood,seeing the Buddha, ... began to utter its melodious notes, as if to praise him. The Buddha, looking back at his disciples, said: "That bird transported with joy at the sight of me unconsciously utters its melodious notes. On account of this good deed, after my passing away this bird shall be born in human form, and named Mātṛceṭa, shall praise my virtues with true appreciation."

Other than these few scraps of information we know nothing of Mātṛceṭa and today his name is remembered only for its association with his greatest work, the Śatapañcāśatka.

The name Śatapañcāśatka literally means "Hymn in a Hundred and Fifty Verses," although there are actually a hundred and fifty-two, or in some versions, a hundred and fifty-three verses in the work. It lies very much within the bhakti or devotional genre of Indian literature but is refreshingly free from the florid style that so often characterises such works. Shackleton-Bailey notes that the "style of the Hymn is simple and direct, free from swollen compounds and elaborate conceits."[2] Warder says that "the restraint of these verses is that of complete mastery of the medium, able to express rich meaning with a few carefully chosen words and without the support of outward display." He goes on to say that the verses "are handled with a kind of reticence suggestive of the poet's humility and detachment, both of which are probably sincere."[3] Certainly all who are familiar with the Hymn in its original Sanskrit acknowledge the great beauty of both its language and meaning. In ancient India numerous commentaries were written on the Hymn. It was popular with the followers of all schools of Buddhism and was translated into several different languages. Tāranātha, the great Tibetan historian, says the Hymn had an important part to play in the spread of Buddhism outside India, and should it become as well known as it once was it may continue to create an interest in the Buddha and his teachings.[4]

Centuries before Mātṛceṭa, the householder Upāli was so inspired by the Buddha's presence that he too composed a hymn of praise. When asked why he had done so he replied:

> "It is as if there were a great heap of different flowers which a clever garland maker or his apprentice might string into a variegated garland. Likewise the Lord has many splendid qualities. And who would not give praise to one worthy of praise?"[5]

There can be no doubt that Mātṛceṭa's hymn likewise is an expression of a deep devotion to the Buddha and an admiration of his qualities. But quite apart from the author's motive in writing it, the value and indeed the purpose of the Hymn to the Buddha is twofold. First it is meant to awaken our faith. Mātṛceṭa recognized as did the Lord himself that faith has the power to arouse a tremendous amount of positive zeal and energy. Long before we have directly experienced it, faith keeps our eyes fixed firmly on the goal. When we stumble and fall, faith picks us up; when doubt causes us to falter, it urges us on; and when we get side-tracked, it brings us back to the Path. Without faith in the Buddha and the efficacy of his

Dharma we would never even bother to try to put the teachings into practice. As Nāgārjuna says:

> One associates with the Dharma out of faith,
> but one knows truly out of understanding;
> understanding is the chief of the two,
> but faith precedes.[6]

The Buddha's qualities are worthy of respect in themselves, but when they are described so fully and so beautifully in verses like those of Mātṛceṭa, our faith can only be strengthened and grow.

The other purpose of the Hymn is to urge us into action. Mātṛceṭa highlights the Buddha's gentleness, his non-retaliation, his patience and his other qualities, knowing that when we have a deep admiration for someone it is natural to try to emulate him. One feels that he used his poetic skills to the full in the hope that we would be inspired enough to make the Buddha our model and follow his example. When we read that the Buddha extended the hand of friendship to all without exception we feel we should try to do the same. On being reminded that the Buddha endured abuse and hardship without complaint we find the strength to be a little more forebearing. When brooding over our imperfections casts us down, nothing fills us with new determination and vigour more than calling to mind the Buddha's attainments. The receptive mind will transform admiration into action.

The Hymn may have another value as well - as an aid to meditation. In concentration meditation thoughts are silenced, in mindfulness meditation they are observed with detachment, but in recollection meditation thoughts are directed to a specific subject which is then carefully pondered upon. The Buddha says: "Monks, whatever a monk ponders on and thinks about often the mind in consequence gets a leaning in that way," and this is certainly true.[7] Any type of thought that is prominent in our mind will have an influence upon our personality and behaviour. To consciously and intentionally think positive thoughts will, in time, allow such thoughts to arise quite naturally, and from that will spring deeds associated with such positive thoughts. In practising the Recollection of the Buddha, *Buddhānussati*, one sits silently, and having made the mind receptive, thinks about the Buddha's many deeds and qualities. In time, faith and devotion, both of which are important spiritual faculties, begin to gain in strength, thus adding energy and even fervour to our practice. Those who do this meditation usually either read or recite the well-known *Iti' pi so* formula to help guide their thoughts. But they may find that reading extracts from the Hymn to the Buddha can be used together with this formula, or at times as a substitute for it, with very positive results.

D.R. Shackleton-Bailey has done a complete English translation of the Hymn to the Buddha and Edward Conze has translated parts of it.[8] Both these translations are literal and scholarly but do not give sufficient regard to the spirit of the work and the author's intention in writing it - to inspire and to uplift. By reworking these two translations and occasionally referring to the Sanskrit text with the help of my friend, Ven. Hippola Paññakithi, I have attempted to produce a readable rendering of this beautiful and important work. Those interested in a scholarly version of the Hymn are advised to read Shackleton-Bailey's translation with its copious notes on language, manuscript variations and textual difficulties.

Hymn to the Buddha

1

Invocation

1   No faults in any way are found in him;
All virtues in every way dwell in him.

2   To go to him for refuge, to sing his praise,
to do him honour and to abide in his Dharma
is proper for one with understanding.

3   The only Protector,
his faults are gone without residue.
The All-knowing One,
his virtues are present without fail.

4   Even the most spiteful man
cannot with justice find fault
in the thoughts, words or deeds of the Lord.

5   To be born human and encounter the great joy
     of the good Dharma is a chance rarer than
     a turtle thrusting its neck through a yoke
     floating freely in the great ocean.

6   So how could I not put voice to good use now,
     for it is impermanent and may soon be liable to change.

7   Though I know that the Sage's virtues
     are beyond all human calculation,
     still I will recount a portion of them,
     if only for my own delight.

8   Homage to you, O Self-developed One
     whose good works are many and wondrous,
     whose virtues are too numerous and awesome to define.

9   Their number? They are infinite.
     Their nature? Words must fail.
     But to speak of them bestows great good,
     so I shall speak much.

2

In Praise of Causes

10   Having brushed aside doubts
      about whether or not it could be done,
      of your own free will you took
      this helpless world under your protection.

11   You were kind without being asked,
      you were loving without reason,
      you were a friend to the stranger
      and a kinsman to those without kin.

12   You gave even your own flesh
      not to mention your wealth and possessions.
      Even your own life's breath, O Kindly One,
      you gave to those who wished for it.[9]

13   A hundred times you ransomed your own body and life
      for the bodies and lives of living beings
      in the grip of their would-be slayers.

14 It was not fear of hell or desire for heaven
    but utter purity of heart
    that made you practise the good.

15 By always avoiding the crooked
    and adhering to the straight,
    you became the highest receptacle for purity.

16 When attacked you used your fiery power
    against the defilements, but in your noble heart
    felt only sympathy for those who were defiled.

17 The joy beings feel on saving their lives
    equals not the joy you experienced
    when you gave your life for others.

18 No matter how often murderers cut you to pieces,
    regardless of the pain
    you felt only compassion for them.

19 That seed of perfect enlightenment,
    that jewel-like mind of yours,
    only you, Great Hero, know its essence.
    Others are far from understanding it.

20 "Nirvāna is not won without perseverance":
    thinking thus you roused great energy
    without a thought for yourself.

21 Your progress towards excellence never faltered
    and now you have attained
    the state that cannot be bettered.

22 But you did not practise in order to experience
the pleasant and fruitful results of meditation.
Always in your heart the motive was compassion.

23 For the happiness which, though sublime,
cannot be shared with others,
pains rather than pleases
those like you, O Righteous One.

24 You imbibed good speech,
bad speech you shunned like poison,
from mixed speech you extracted what was sweet.[10]

25 Purchasing words of wisdom even with your own life,
in birth after birth, O Knower of Gems,
you were zealous for enlightenment.

26 Thus striving through the three incalculable aeons
accompanied only by your resolution,
you gained the highest state.[11]

3

In Praise of Incomparability

27   By not envying the superior,
      despising the inferior,
      or competing with equals,
      you attained pre-eminence in the world.

28   You were devoted to virtues for their own sake,
      not for the rewards that come from them,
      and thus due to your right progress
      they have all come to completion within you.

29   So much good have you gathered by your deeds
      that even the dust on your feet
      has become a source of merit.

30   You dissolved and uprooted your faults,
      you purified and brought to completion your virtues,
      and by this wise procedure
      you reached the highest attainment.

31   You struck at faults with your might
      so that not even their shadow
      lingers in the depths of your mind.[12]

32   Step by step you nurtured the virtues
      and established them in yourself, so that now
      not even their likeness is found elsewhere.

33   All worldly objects of comparison
      can be damaged or obstructed,
      limited by time and space, easily acquired.

34   How can they be compared with your virtues --
      virtues unrivalled, unapproachable,
      stable, unceasing, unsurpassed?

35   When measured against the unfathomable
      and boundless depth of your understanding,
      the ocean becomes as if a mere puddle.

36   When matched with your calm equanimity,
      the firmness of the earth
      seems like the quivering of a flower petal.

37   Beside the radiance of your wisdom,
      which destroys the darkness of ignorance,
      the sun does not attain even the brightness of a firefly.

38   The purity of the moon, the sky or a pool in autumn
      appears clouded when compared
      with the purity of your words, thoughts and deeds.

39 I have compared you with all that is admired in the world,
but still how far are those miserable things
from the qualities of a Buddha.

40 For there is only one thing that resembles you,
O Kindly One, and that is the jewel of the Dharma
through which you attained the highest.

41 But if something were to be found comparable to you,
to make such comparison
would be the act of a foolish and disrespectful man.

4

In Praise of Wonders

42   Your victory over Māra evokes wonder in people
but considering your great virtues
I think this is but a minor thing.[13]

43   Even those who lash out in fury to assault you
are not a heavy burden for your patience to bear
housed as it is in such a worthy vessel.

44   What is truly wondrous is this:
after you conquered Māra, on that same night
you were able to conquer your own defilements.

45   He who is amazed at your victory over opponents,
might well be amazed at the sun for dispelling the darkness
with its garland of a thousand rays.

46   You have overcome three things with three things:
passion with passionlessness,
anger with love,
and ignorance with wisdom.

47   Good deeds you praise, bad deeds you blame,
      but towards those who act thus
      you are free from any "for" or "against."

48   Is any praise high enough for you
      whose mind transcends
      attachment to the noble and dislike for the ignoble?[14]

49   You did not cling to virtue
      nor yearn for those who were virtuous.
      Ah! See the purity of this most tranquil being!

50   How permanently calm your mind is can be known
      by seeing how unalterably calm your senses are.

51   Even the foolish acknowledge the purity of your mind.
      The goodness of your words and deeds
      reflects your pure thoughts.

5

In Praise of Form

52 Lovely yet calming, bright but not blinding, gentle
    yet strong. Who would not be inspired just to see you?

53 The joy one feels on beholding you for the first time
    does not diminish even after seeing you a hundred times.

54 Each time it is seen, your form gives joy;
    its beauty is such that one is never satisfied.

55 Your body is worthy as a receptacle
    and your virtues are worthy as occupants.
    Both are excellent in themselves
    and both complement each other perfectly.

56 Where else could the virtues of a Tathāgata
    be so well housed as in your body,
    shining as it does with auspicious marks and signs?[15]

57   Your body seems to say to your virtues:
      "I am blessed to have you,"
     and your virtues seem to respond:
     "Where better could we dwell?"

6

In Praise of Compassion

58   You long bound yourself to compassion in order to free
all those in the world who were bound by defilements.

59   Which shall I praise first, you or the great compassion
by which you were long held in saṁsāra
though well you knew its faults?[16]

60   Although you preferred the delights of solitude,
compassion led you to spend your time among the crowd.

61   Like a mighty dragon drawn from its lake by a spell,
compassion led you from forest to town
for the sake of those to be taught.

62   Though abiding in deep tranquillity, the development of
compassion made you take up even the musical art.[17]

63   Your powers, your lion's roar
and the manifestation of virtues are but glitter
rubbed off the nugget of your innate compassion.[18]

64   Your compassion was kind only towards others,
      but was cruel towards her own master.
      Towards you alone, O Lord, compassion was pitiless.[19]

65   That same compassion
      had you cut into a hundred pieces
      and cast you like an offering to the four quarters,
      all for the sake of others.

66   But clearly compassion always acted in accordance
      with your will. For although she oppressed you,
      she did not transgress against your desires.

7

In Praise of Speech

67-8 Well worded and significant, true and sweet,
    deep or plain or both together, condensed or copious.
    Hearing such words of yours, would not even an opponent
    be convinced that you were all-knowing?

69   Generally your speech was wholly sweet
    but when necessary it would be otherwise.
    But either way, every word was well spoken
    because it always achieved its purpose.

70   Soft or hard or possessing both qualities,
    all your words when distilled had but one taste.[20]

71   Ah! How pure, perfect and excellent your actions are,
    that you employed these jewel-like words in such a way.

72   From your mouth pleasing to the eye, drop words
    pleasing to the ear, like nectar from the moon.[21]

73   Your sayings are like a spring shower
      settling the dust of passions,
      like a garuda killing the serpent of hatred.[22]

74   They are like the sun again and again
      dispelling the darkness of ignorance,
      like Śakra's sceptre splitting the mountain of pride.[23]

75   Your speech is excellent in three ways:
      based on fact it is truthful,
      because its motive is pure it causes no confusion,
      and being relevant it is easily understood.

76   When first heard your words excite the mind
      but when their meaning is pondered over
      they wash away all ignorance and passion.

77   They go to the hearts of all.
      While comforting the grieving they alarm the heedless
      and rouse those preoccupied with pleasures.

78   Truly your words are for all: they delight the wise,
      strengthen those of middling intelligence
      and illuminate the minds of the dull.

79   Your sayings coax men from false views
      and draw them towards Nirvāna.
      They remove faults and rain down virtues.

80   Your knowledge embraces all things,
      your mindfulness is ever present
      and thus what you say will always come to pass.

81　Because you never speak at the wrong time
　　or in the wrong place or towards the wrong person,
　　your words, like energy rightly applied, are never wasted.

8

In Praise of Teaching

82   Your dispensation and only yours is the true path:
its methods are pleasant, its fruits good,
it is free from faults and lovely
in the beginning, the middle and the end.[24]

83   If fools, because of their attachment to deluded views,
condemn your wonderful teaching,
then deluded views are their own worst enemy.

84   Remembering the suffering which you endured
for the sake of others, it would be good
to listen to your teachings even if they were wrong.

85   But coming from one so kind in words and deeds,
how much more should your teachings be practised
with all the vigour one would use to remove
a blazing turban from one's head.

86 Freedom, the joy of enlightenment,
   praiseworthy virtues and peace:
   these four benefits are all gained from your teaching.

87 O Great Hero, your teachings brought trembling to
        sectarians,
   misery to Namuci, but rejoicing to both gods and men.[25]

88 Even the rule of Death, which extends
   without impediment or obstacle over the triple world,
   has been crushed by your teaching.[26]

89 For those who fathom your teachings can live an aeon
   if they so desire, but freely they depart
   to the realm where death cannot tread.[27]

90 Only in your dispensation is time divided
   for studying the scriptures, pondering their meaning
   and practising meditation.

91 What is more distressful than this, Great Sage,
   that some people do not revere your teaching,
   full of goodness as it is?

9

In Praise of Benefits Conferred

92   Just to hear you brings joy;
just to look upon you calms the heart;
your speech refreshes and your teaching frees.

93   People rejoice at your birth,
they celebrate as you grow,
they benefit from your presence
and sorrow in your absence.

94   To praise you removes faults,
to recollect you brings joy,
to follow you gives understanding,
to know you purifies the heart.

95   To approach you brings good fortune,
to serve you gives wisdom,
to worship you dispels fear,
to wait upon you bestows prosperity .

96   You are a great lake of goodness,
with waters purified by virtue,
surface calmed by meditation
and depths stilled by wisdom.

97   Your form is a jewel to see,
your speech is a jewel to hear,
your teachings are a jewel to reflect upon.
Truly, you are a mine bearing the jewels of goodness.

98   You are an island for those swept along by the flood,
a shelter for the stricken,
a refuge for those in fear of becoming,
a resort for those who aspire to liberation.

99   To all living beings
you are a useful vessel because of your virtue,
a fertile field because of your perfect fruit,
a true friend because of the benefits you confer.

100   You are admired for your altruism,
charming for your tenderness,
beloved for your gentleness
and honoured for your many virtues.

101   You are cherished because of your flawlessness,
delightful because of the goodness of your form and
      speech,
opulent because you promote the good of all,
and blessed because you are the abode of virtues.

10

In Praise of Guidance

102-3 You admonish the stubborn,
restrain the hasty and straighten the crooked.
You encourage the slow and harness the tamed.
Truly, you are the unsurpassed guide of men.

104 You have pity for the suffering, good-will for the happy,
compassion for the distressed, benevolence for all.

105 The hostile evoke your warmth,
the immoral receive your help, the fierce find you tender.
How wonderful is your noble heart!

106 If father and mother are to be honoured
because of concern for their children,
what reverence should you receive
whose love has no limits?

107 You are a wall of safety
for those hovering at the edge of the cliff,
those blind to their own welfare,
those who are their own worst enemy.

108 For the welfare of the two worlds
and to help beings transcend them,
you lit the lamp of wisdom
among those who dwell in darkness.[28]

109 When worldly enjoyments are at stake,
men and gods act at variance with each other.
But because they can enjoy the Dharma in harmony,
they are reconciled in you.

110 O Blessed One, you have given the comfort
of the Dharma unstintingly to all,
regardless of birth, age or caste,
regardless of time or place.

111 As if amazed and envious
the gods honour with joined palms even your disciples,
who unlike them are free from amazement and envy.

112 Ah! How brilliant is the arising of a Buddha,
that cream of saṁsāra.
Because of him the gods envy mankind.

11

In Praise of Arduous Deeds

113   Fatigue, loss of the joy of solitude,
      the company of fools, the press of the crowd
      and the pairs of opposites: all these discomforts
      you endure as if they were blessings.[29]

114   With mind detached, you quietly work
      for the welfare of the world.
      How awesome is the Buddha-nature of the Buddha![30]

115   You ate poor food, sometimes you went hungry.
      You walked rough paths and slept on the ground
      trampled hard by the hooves of cattle.[31]

116   Though you are the Master, in order to serve others
      you endured insults and adapted your clothes and words,
      out of love for those whom you taught.

117   You are the Lord, but you never lord it over others.
      All may use you as a servant to obtain the help they need.

118 No matter who provoked you,
where or how, never did you transgress
your own path of fair conduct.

119 You help those who wish you ill
more than most men
help those who wish them well.

120 To an enemy intent on evil
you are a friend intent on good.
To one who gleefully seeks faults
you respond by seeking virtues.

121 Those who sought to give you poison and fire
you approached with compassion and nectar.

122 You conquered revilers with patience,
the malicious with blessings,
slanderers with truth and the cruel with kindness.

123 You reversed in an instant
the manifold natures and evil destinies
of those depraved from beginningless time.

12

In Praise of Skill

124 Through your skill in teaching the rough became gentle,
the mean became generous and the cruel became kind.

125 A Nanda became serene, a Mānastabdha humble,
an Aṅgulīmāla compassionate.
Who would not be amazed?[32]

126 Delighted with the flavour of your teaching,
many wise ones left their beds of gold
to sleep on beds of straw.

127 Because you knew time and temperaments,
sometimes you remained silent when questioned,
sometimes you spoke first, and at other times
you aroused their interest and then spoke.

128 Having first scrubbed clean the garment of the mind
with talk on generosity and other virtues,
you then applied the dye of the Dharma.

129　There is no expedient or opportunity
　　　which you did not use
　　　in order to rescue this pitiful world
　　　from the fearful abyss of saṁsāra.

130　To train people in different situations,
　　　according to their state of mind,
　　　many and various were the words and deeds you used.

131　They were pure and friendly, honoured and praised,
　　　saluted and acclaimed by both gods and men.

132　Difficult it is to speak well and then do good.
　　　But for you, O Truthful One, both these things come easily.

133　By your purity alone you could have cleansed the
　　　　　whole universe.
　　　In the triple world no one is to be found like you.

134　You rose up for the welfare of all beings
　　　lost in the beginningless and fearful straits of becoming.

13

In Praise of Freedom from Debt

135 I know not how to repay you
for what you have done;
even those who have attained Nirvāna
are still in your debt.

136 Established in the Dharma by you,
they accomplished their own welfare only.
But you worked by yourself for the welfare of all,
so how can you be repaid for that?

137 You look upon those who slumber and gently awaken
them.
You are a kind and heedful friend to those who are
heedless.

138 You have declared the destruction of the defilements,
you have exposed Māra's delusions,
you have taught the evils of saṁsāra,
you have revealed the place without fear.

139 Those who work for the welfare of the world
     and those of compassionate heart, what could they do
     wherein you have not already led the way?

140 If your good qualities could be given to others,
     surely you would have shared them with all,
     even with Devadatta.[33]

141 Out of compassion for the world
     you promoted the good Dharma for so long on earth.
     Many disciples have you raised
     capable of working for the welfare of the world.[34]

142 Many personal converts have you trained,
     Subhadra being the last.
     What still remains of your debt to living beings?[35]

143 Powdering your bones into tiny pieces
     with the diamond of concentration, even in the end
     you continued to do what was hard to do.

144 "My Dharma body and my physical body both exist
     only for the sake of others." Speaking thus
     even in Nirvāna you taught this reluctant world.[36]

145 Having given your entire Dharma body to the virtuous,
     you broke your physical body into fragments
     and attained final Nirvāna.

146 What steadfastness! What conduct!
     What form! What virtue!
     Truly there is nothing about the Buddha's qualities
     that is not wonderful.

147 Yet even to you whose speech and actions are so
      helpful
    are some men hostile. Behold the ferocity of delusion!

148 O ocean of good, treasury of gems,
    heap of merit, mine of virtues!
    Those who honour you are themselves worthy of honour.

149 Your virtues are limitless
    but my capacity to praise them is not.
    Therefore I shall finish, not because I am satisfied
    but for fear of running out of words.

150 Only you can measure your own qualities
    being as they are beyond measure,
    beyond number, thought and comparison.

151 I have hardly begun to sing your praise
    and yet already my heart is filled with joy.
    But need a lake be drained
    before one's thirst be quenched?

152 Through the merit arising from my good deed,
    born of faith in the Sage,
    may the minds of beings now tossed by evil thoughts
    be free from distress and come to peace.

NOTES

All references to the Pāli Nikāyas are to volume and page number of the Pali Text Society editions.

1   A. K. Warder, *Indian Kāvya Literature* (Delhi, 1974), Vol. II, Chapter 7, contains a detailed and informative analysis of the style, contents and alliterations in Mātṛceṭa's works and of their place in the Indian Kāvya tradition.

2   D. R. Shackleton-Bailey, *The Śatapañcāśatka of Mātṛceṭa* (Cambridge, 1951).

3   *Indian Kāvya Literature*, Vol. II, p.234.

4   Lama Chimpa and Alaka Chattopadhayaya, *Tāranātha's History of Buddhism in India* (Calcutta, 1980), Chapter 18.

5   Majjhima Nikāya, II:387.

6   Ratnavālī 5.

7   Majjhima Nikāya, II:115.

8   Edward Conze, *Buddhist TextsThrough the Ages* (New York, 1954).

9   Here and in verses 13, 17 and 18 reference is to the Buddha sacrificing his life in former births as recounted in the Jātaka Stories.

10   A mixture of truth and falsehood, useful and useless.

11   It is said to take a bodhisattva at least three incalculable aeons to attain full enlightenment. See Har Dayal, *The Bodhisattva Doctrine in Buddhist Sanskrit Literature* (London, 1932).

12   *Ātmasamtāne*: literally, "the flow (of consciousness) that makes up the self." Pāli, *cittasantati.*

13   *Māra*: evil personified, the Tempter in Buddhism.

14   *Arhat*: literally, a saint. *Tīrthika*: an adherent of a non-Buddhist sect.

15   *Tathāgata*: An epithet of the Buddha meaning the "Thus Come One" or the "Thus Gone One." The thirty-two major marks and the eighty minor signs are special features of a Buddha's physical body.

16   *Saṁsāra*: the beginningless round of birth and death.

17   In one of his former lives the Buddha was born as a musician and used his skills to convert the gods. See Guttila Jātaka.

18   On the ten psychic powers, see Nyānatiloka, *Buddhist Dictionary* (Colombo, 1972) under *Iddhi*. The "lion's roar" is the Buddha's bold and confident claim to enlightenment. The meaning of this verse is that compassion, the nugget, is the most important thing while the powers, etc., "the glitter," are just a by-product of that compassion.

19   Here and in verses 65 and 66 compassion is personified as one who acts for the sake of others even to the extent of causing discomfort to the Buddha.

20   The taste of liberation (*vimuttirasa*) - Udāna 56.

21   The ancient Indians believed that nectar fell from the moon.

22   The *garuda* is a mythological bird, the natural enemy of the serpent.

23   *Śakra* is the king of the gods in Vedic mythology. He has a scepter of unbreakable hardness.

24   *Ekāyanam*: literally, the one way, thus "the true path."

25   *Namuci*: another name for Māra.

26   The triple world: the world of desire, the world of form and the formless world. See *Buddhist Dictionary* under *Loka.*

27   For the notion that those who have mastered the teaching can live for an aeon, see Dīgha Nikāya, II: 103, 118.

28   The "two worlds" are the world of gods and the world of humans.

29   The pairs of opposites are praise and blame, cold and heat, sickness and health, ease and discomfort, etc.

30   *Buddhadharmatā.* See *Encyclopedia of Buddhism*, Vol. III (Colombo, 1973), p.435.

31 For a description of the hardships and simplicity of the Buddha's life similar to those mentioned here, see Anguttara Nikāya, I:34.

32 Nanda was so distracted by sensual thoughts that he was unable to meditate - Udāna 21. Mānastabdha was so proud that he would not even respect his parents - Saṁyutta Nikāya, I:177. Aṅgulīmāla was a terrible murderer - Majjhima Nikāya, II: 98-103. All were skilfully transformed by the Buddha.

33 Devadatta was the Buddha's evil cousin who caused a schism in the monastic community and even tried to kill the Buddha.

34 Shackleton-Bailey includes, prior to this verse, a verse of which he notes that its grammatical peculiarities and exclusion from early texts are "sufficiently strong grounds for doubting its authenticity." I have therefore decided to omit it.

35 As he lay on his death-bed the Buddha taught and made a disciple of Subhadra. See Dīgha Nikāya, II:149, 153.

36 Here and in verse 145 the Buddha's teaching or Dharma body, which lasts as long as people understand and practise his teachings, is compared with his physical body which disintegrates at death. See I. B. Horner's discussion on *dhammakāya* in *Milinda's Questions* (London, 1963), p:xl

AVAILABLE FROM BPS

THE BUDDHA AND HIS TEACHINGS

Mahāthera Nārada

Since its first appearance in 1964, the Ven.Mahāthera Nārada's *The Buddha and His Teachings* has come to be regarded as one of the clearest and most detailed introductions to the fundamental teachings of Buddhism available in English.

In simple and lucid language the Ven.Nārada explains those doctrines and concepts which form the common bedrock of all Buddhism, as they have been preserved by the oldest surviving school, the Theravāda.

The first part of his work is devoted to the life of the Buddha, with separate chapters on the Buddha's relatives, his supporters and opponents, his outstanding disciples, his ministry and his passing away. The remainder of the book explains in detail the Buddha's teachings, exploring such basic Buddhist doctrines as the Four Noble Truths, kamma and rebirth, Nibbāna, and the practice of meditation. The final chapters show the continuing relevance of Buddhism of the problems of modern life.

400 pages
Softback

THE BUDDHIST PUBLICATION SOCIETY

is an approved charity dedicated to making known the Teaching of the Buddha, which has a vital message for people of all creeds.

Founded in 1958, the BPS has published a wide variety of books and booklets covering a great range of topics. Its publications include accurate annotated translations of the Buddha's discourses, standard reference works, as well as original contemporary expositions of Buddhist thought and practice. These works present Buddhism as it truly is --a dynamic force which has influenced receptive minds for the past two thousand years and is still as relevant today as it was when it first arose.

A full list of our publications will be sent free of charge upon request. Write to:

The Hony. Secretary
BUDDHIST PUBLICATION SOCIETY
P. O. Box 61
54, Sangharaja Mawata
Kandy Sri Lanka